To my Family

To my Family	0
DADDY AND I	5
UNCLE ROMANO	11
AT GRANDMA PEPPINA'S	14
AT THE NEIGHBOUR'S	19
MUM AND SUNDAY	22
AT AGNESE'S	25
CROCHET AT GRANDMA'S	28
SHOES WITH HEELS AND IRON SHAVINGS	33
MY BEST FRIEND	37
THE VINTAGE TURNTABLE	41
THE ROCKING HORSE AND BOXING LESSONS	44
TRAVELLING BY CAR WITH THE PORTABLE RECORD PLAYER	47
THE SWING BETWEEN THE OLIVE TREES	50
DO NOT STEAL	53
GRANDFATHER ARMANDO	56
THE WOODEN CLOGS	58
THE SEA IN SEPTEMBER	60
THE HARVEST	63
LONDON-MAY 2020-LOCKDOWN	67
SUMMER 1983	71

Sonja Taggiasco

BREAD, BUTTER and SUGAR

Copyright 2020 © Sonja Taggiasco
First Edition 2020

Illustration by Sonja Taggiasco

Summer 1977

DADDY AND I

I'm ready, I'm waiting for Dad downstairs at my great-grandmother's house.

I turn the soapy water in the plastic cup that my grandmother prepared for me.

I also have a new hollow cane. Dad prepared it for me yesterday, a super cane, green and smooth to make super soap bubbles.

Today I am in the canoe, in the stream, making bubbles

"Come on let's go," says Dad.

I watch him and I giggle. I like to go with him to the field where we grow vegetables. While he works the land, I spend time on my canoe.

It's not a real canoe, it is a large canoe-shaped stone in the middle of the water. But for me it's the same, even if it doesn't move, it's like being on a boat.

We made the journey in the Ape, which is a small vehicle that my dad sometimes uses to go to the field, which is close to home. We have already arrived.

The sun is high in the sky. It's a hot day so I put on a flowered hat. I take Daddy's hand and we go down into the field.

The crickets sing, almost in an uproar, in the silence of the countryside.

"Will you carry me to the canoe Daddy?"
He always carries me in his arms so I don't get wet.

The water isn't high, it's only a small stream, but Daddy wears boots, the ones you wear even when it rains.
He leaves me sitting in the middle of that big stone with my soap bubbles.
"Call me when you want to leave," he says.

I look at him but I don't really see him, just a shadow above me with a mane of blond hair lit by the sun, but I know he is smiling, I can hear it in his voice.
And with three steps he is out of the water.
I see him walking on the bank and climbing up into the first strip of land where he starts working.

I sit here, a light breeze moves my hat, I press it down and I mix the soap in the glass.
I narrow my eyes to observe through my lashes the reflection of the sun in the water.

It moves, relentlessly, shining a thousand bright dots chasing each other.
The air is cooler here, under the shade of trees, I put a hand in the water, it is chilly and clear.
A few insects move on the surface, they walk on the water drawing small circles with their tiny legs that seem to have round paws at the end.

How they manage not to sink is a mystery to me.

They don't scare me, I'm used to the countryside, but I don't like them enough to touch them.

The bubbles don't work, when we go back I have to ask my great-grandmother for more pieces of soap.

She told me that laundry soap is better for making bubbles, but that's not true.

I would like some of that for washing up, but it seems as precious as Parmigiano Reggiano cheese.

Even when I ask my grandmother for a little of this cheese, she cuts me a slice that is almost transparent and you don't have time to taste it.

Only mum gives me a real piece that you can bite, chew and taste.

My fake canoe trip today bores me a bit with these bubbles that don't work.

I call dad, he picks me up and takes me with him.

I look for earthworms while I'm waiting for Dad to finish working the land, I find some under a stone.

Earthworms are cold and a little wet, like the soil under the stone, they are smooth and soft and eat the soil, then they poop, which is not really poop, it is the soil they have eaten but much thinner.

This is what they do, they work the land like dad does with the machine, but they use their bodies.

8

Now the sun is setting, I take off my hat and I get some goosebumps on my arms.

I run up to the last strip where Dad is.
That machine makes a lot of noise, I've already called him three times but he doesn't hear me.
I wait here sitting on the steps of the last strip by the road.

I see a cricket, one of those who makes great leaps and has wings that open between one jump and another.
The wings can either be blue or red.

Once I grabbed so many that there was no space left in my hands and they started kicking with those slightly pungent legs, that scared me and I screamed as I opened my hands to let them go.
After that day I didn't catch any more.

We went back and stopped by my great-grandmother.

I don't call her great-grandmother, it's a word too long to say, I call her grandmother Adalgisa and even when I say it, it still seems very long.

Grandma is enough for me but then if my grandmothers are together and they answer at the same time, confusion is created.
So I have grandmother Adalgisa and grandmother Peppina who is my great-grandmother's daughter.

My great-grandmother made me bread with butter and sugar, it's a very sweet snack but I like it.

Sometimes at the first bite my cheeks hurt.
I could ask for bread with oil and vinegar that I like better, but today it was ready with a glass of water and mint syrup.

My great-grandmother puts so much syrup that the water is dark green.

But the darker green happens when she makes the vegetable soup.

My favorite soup, delicious, very green as if there were all the different shades of green in the world, mixed together, and there are no pieces in it.
Super good, nobody can make it as good as this one, not even grandmother Peppina, who is her daughter.

"Do you want to go upstairs to sprinkle salt on the tomatoes?" she asks me.
Yes, I want to go. I love the smell of chopped tomatoes left drying in the sun.
And I also like dried tomatoes when they are ready to be eaten.

We go up to the attic, then from the attic we go to this small terrace which is right on top of the house.
I can already smell the tomatoes before opening the door.

UNCLE ROMANO

When we go to park the vehicle at my grandmother's house, Uncle Romano is there.

He is the tallest in the family, but he doesn't have a lot of hair on the top of his head and he would like to have more.

I know because I see that he lets the hairs grow very long on one side of his head and then he turns them on the top to cover the space where the hair is missing and when it's windy he has to keep moving them to put them back on his head.

Maybe I should lend him two hairclips of mine, but he is beautiful anyway and the best at making me fly in the air.

In fact I can't wait.
"Hi Uncle" my voice trills.
"Hi Sonja!"

And he already knows it, so he gets ready, his body a little bent with his arms spread and I run fast until my body meets his arms and he throws me into the air.

It's a beautiful feeling, I go really high and every time I hope my uncle catches me when I go down.

But until now he has always caught me and made me fly again and again.
Then he goes back to wash his sporty car which is pea green colour and asks me: "Do you want to come to Sant'Ampelio beach with me later?"

At Sant 'Ampelio seafront there are only rocks, but the water is so transparent that you can see everything underneath, which is fortunate because in this way you also can avoid putting your feet on sea urchins.

I have to use water wings to swim because there is no place where you can touch the bottom, but my uncle always swims close to me and then takes me back to the rocks and goes for a long swim.

I say that I want to go with him, so that he will come to pick me up later.

Uncle Romano

AT GRANDMA PEPPINA'S

Today I am with my grandmother, the sky is grey and it's raining.

Grandma is a little chubby and she is serious most of the time , perhaps sad.

Maybe she's just sad because she no longer has her husband who would have been my grandfather, my dad's dad.

I never knew my grandfather and he didn't spend a long time with his family because he died when my dad was 10 years old.

This thing scares me a little, a young dad who suddenly dies. I don't tell anyone, but I do think about it.

I have not reached ten years old yet so the thought that something can happen when I reach that age comes every now and again.

Sometimes I'm worried if dad or mum are late, because I don't know if something may have happened.

Today with the rain my cousin Dimitri and I could build a hut made of umbrellas and stay inside the shelter for a while.

If his mum lets him out and isn't scolding him as usual.

When she scolds him, which is practically every day, she says to him "Come here, now, I put oil on you!" but I

don't understand why she wants to put oil on him and above all, which type of oil would she use?
What punishment is it?

But when he comes out to play he is never oiled, or he has not been oiled or he has, and he has been washed off before his mum let him out.

So today, again, we collect all the umbrellas available, we open them and we sit down to listen to the rain.

Myself and Dimitri

This is a game that cannot last very long, because it's boring after a while.

When the rain stops we go up to the bridge that leads to the road to see if those tiny frogs that move in leaps have come out.

They are grey in colour and they blend in with the asphalt, so you have to sit there for a while trying to see them.

They blend perfectly, you only see them if they make a small leap.

We find some of them and we put them in the garden in a jar to swim, but obviously we forget them.

I go home to my grandmother and go to the terrace, the one overlooking the stream.

There is a closet where I keep some toys, but today a very bad surprise awaits me.

"Nonnaaaaa!" I call her.
"Come and see Melina's face," I say.

Melina is a small doll with very long hair that I like so much but today she no longer has one her cheeks and there are bite marks

My grandmother inspects the doll and says "A mouse ate her cheek".

And she tells me in a way as if nothing had happened to Melina.

"You can play with her anyway," she adds.

What? She can't see the gravity of the situation: the doll is disfigured.

It had already been a shock to find my blonde Barbie, which I keep at Agnese's house, with her legs detached.

Dad had fixed it by putting a pin that held her legs together, and I had pretended that she had had an accident skiing and I always keep her dressed, so I don't see the pin.

But Melina without a cheek? There is nothing to do here, she will be without a cheek forever even if I comb her hair forward.

I go back downstairs to the garden and see Carlo who went to visit his grandmother.
I smile "Now I will have a laugh" I think.
Because Carlo is afraid of everything.

I pick a snail and hide it in my hand.
" Carlo? Come downstairs!" I call him.
He is on the terrace looking at me.
"Okay," he says.
I meet him at the gate of his grandmother's house.
"Come and see, I have a surprise" I tell him.
"What is it ?" he asks me.
"If I tell you it's no longer a surprise," I reply.

I put my hands behind my back and say "Guess which hand?

He doesn't guess straight away and I move that snail in my hands several times, my hands are now sticky.

In the end he guesses and I open my hand in front of his nose and he almost screams and runs away.
Even a snail scared him.

Before I put the snail back on the ground, I brush the antennas one by one to see that it is retracting and stretching them back again.
On top of the antennas it has tiny black balls but I don't think they are eyes.

I go back to my grandmother laughing and tell her about the snail and she laughs too.

AT THE NEIGHBOUR'S

Today our neighbour Pierina is babysitting me.
She is a very small woman, just a bit taller than me.
Dad said that when she was a child, she fell out of a highchair, hurt her back and she stopped growing.

I don't like her soup at all, giant pieces of onion float on it, I just can't eat it.
Sometimes I am forced to eat the soup and while I eat it I remove all the pieces I see.

But sometimes it makes me almost puke so I tell her that I cannot have it because I'm sick.
One evening, after using that excuse for not eating the soup, I was starving and after a while I asked her to make me a steak, so she knew I was telling her a lie and told my mum.

On her balcony, I have a little ball to play with, but I have to be very careful not to hit the geraniums that are in pots all along the terrace.

I prefer to play in the square which is just outside the front door but there are no children playing there right now.
Maybe later.
I get bored because Pierina doesn't play any games with me.

I sit next to the geraniums and decide to put polish on the nail using the petals of the pinkest geranium.

I pull the petals one by one, lick them and stick them on my fingernails.

When I'm almost done and I have only two nails left, Pierina comes out to check what I'm doing and she is not happy with what she sees, she scolds me.

How boring!

I take off the petals and they all stick to the tiles and stain them red, so I go to get some toilet paper and clean the tiles before Pierina comes back to check on me again.

There are other plants at the bottom of the terrace.
These flowers are pink balls and I crush them between my fingers to make them plop, hoping that no one notices it this time.
No fun today, I look forward to my mum coming back from work, hoping she bought me the weekly Mickey Mouse comics.

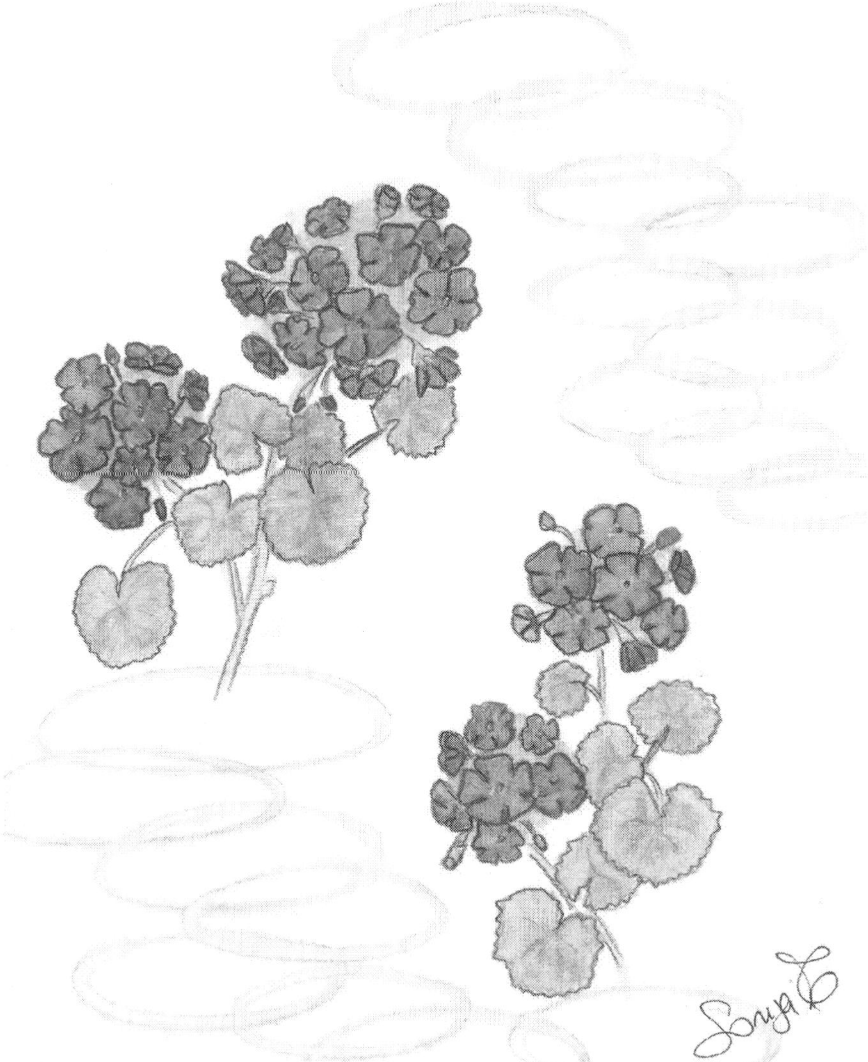

MUM AND SUNDAY

My mum is too young to know how to make a good meal.
She cooks when she's off from work but I don't taste that good flavour like when I eat at my grandmother's.
Sometimes it's good though.

Anyway, she's shouting from the kitchen now to tell me to get ready to go to mass.
Nobody in my family goes to mass.
Just me, because mum forces me and when I ask her why, she says I have to go because she would have wanted to go as a child and her mum didn't send her.
I still don't understand the meaning of it but I start to make the bed.
I drag myself out of the room.

It is Sunday and therefore mum doesn't go to work, instead she is cleaning, sweeping and dusting the house.
Unfortunately I do not notice a small mound of dust in the middle of the room ready to be collected with the dustpan.

I walk on it and it's not the first time for me, so I already know what's going to happen and I start to run out the front door while mum starts screaming and obviously chasing me.
She throws her slippers at me and I laugh and run away.

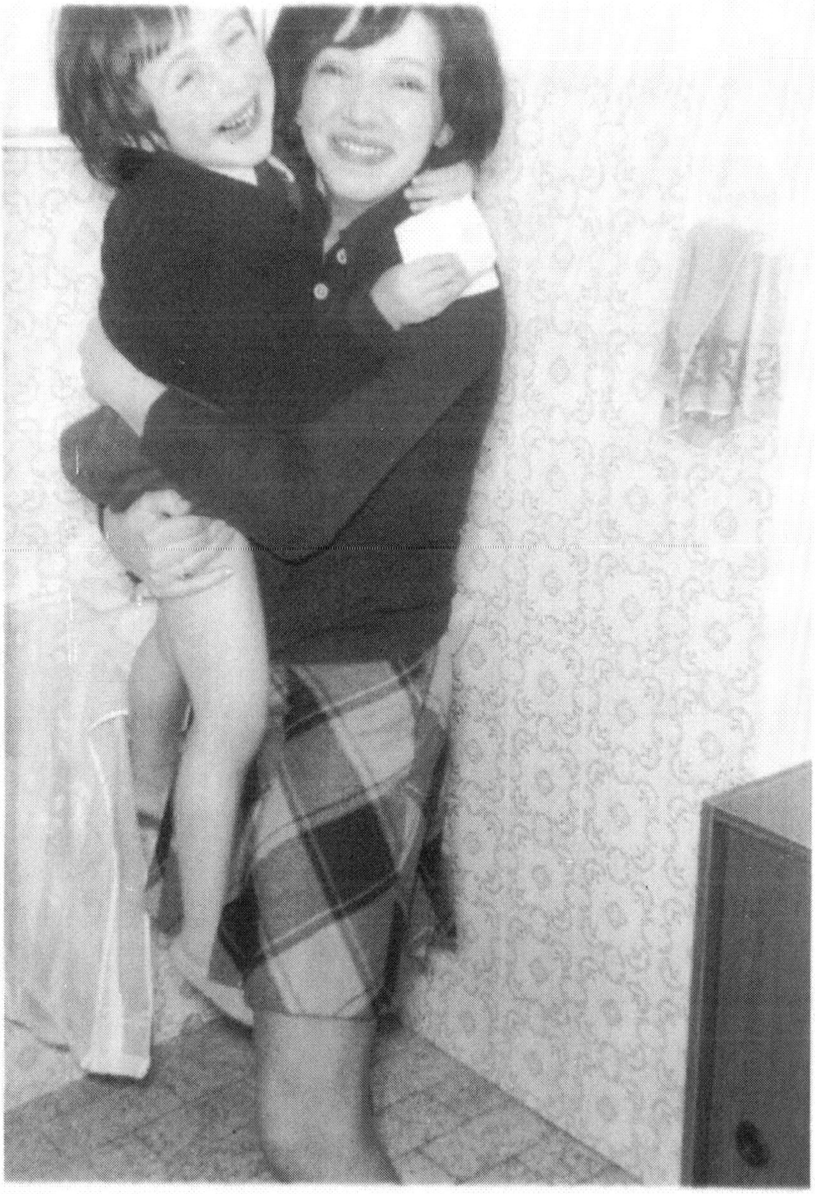

She never catches me, because she doesn't really try, she just does a little drama and then she calms down and starts singing "Pink flowers, peach flowers".

I go back home, get ready and go to mass wearing a "Sunday dress"", with black patent leather shoes that hurt my feet and white socks with lace.

In the church, every now and again I start laughing, maybe because I have to be serious and I don't like too many rules.

If the priest notices me laughing, he looks at me a bit angry and I try to get serious again.

The best moment is when everyone starts singing and then I also sing out loud.

I also like queuing to take the communion but first you have to confess, and when I go to confession I invent something because I have no great sins to confess.

To the priest I say:

"Yesterday I ate the jam and mum told me not to eat it" but I didn't eat any jam, I just say it to take communion.

At the next confession I should say that I tell the lies to the parish priest.

The priest also drinks a lot of wine during the mass but he does not offer any to us sinners.

AT AGNESE'S

Agnese is another woman who takes care of me when mum goes to work, she is another neighbour.
    She lives with her husband, he goes hunting and brings the birds that Agnese cooks and I have to eat.

    There is not a lot of meat attached to those tiny bodies, and they make me feel a bit sorry, but the taste is quite good.
    She crushes that tiny head and makes me suck the brain which she says is good for me.

    It is not the only brain that she makes me eat, she also cooks the cow's brain which is then seasoned with oil and lemon. I don't dislike it, better than the soup with the floating pieces.

    And then every evening she goes to mass for vespers.
    Sometimes I go too, I sit on the bench with her but I don't understand what she whispers all the time and she whispers a lot.

    Kneeling on the bench I only make the noise of the whisper because I really have no idea what to say during that moment, then my knees start to hurt and I can't wait for the priest to say: "Stand up!"

27

I look at Agnese kneeling next to me, her eyes closed, her hands clasped and a black lace on her head.

After the vespers we go home.

When we wait for mum to come home from work, Agnese sometimes makes me slide-row on her legs and always makes the joke of staying still and pretending to be dead.
I know she's alive, but it's not a nice joke because she's old and you never know if her eyes may reopen every time.
While I wait patiently for Agnese to come back to life, I really observe her closely.

The holes where she puts the earrings are two eyelets, really elongated holes, maybe those earrings weigh a lot.
Then I see blue veins under her skin near the temples, and the white hair is pulled back and held in a curl behind the neck.

She also has a necklace with a medal with a saint.

And then she invariably says "Boo!" and opens her eyes but I'm not scared anymore.
I recognize the noise of Mum's car and wait to hear the steps on the staircase, I finally go home.

CROCHET AT GRANDMA'S

There are days like today that never seem to end, we are still sitting on the marble steps of the entrance to my great-grandmother's house and it is almost evening.

Since this afternoon after lunch, we are all here with the crochet hooks still in our hands: me, mum and grandmother Adalgisa.

Grandma is very good with crochet, she does things that seem machine-made: blankets, doilies, jackets, she can do anything.
Mum is quite good, she is learning.

Today I made so many hats for Barbie, my grandmother taught me how to make them but she gave me some wool with colours that I don't like.

The sun is setting but it is still hot, it feels good out here.

Above us are all vine leaves that have climbed up to create a roof.

Every now and again the cat comes close to where we are, I put down the crochet hook and slowly I try to touch him, but when I am close enough to reach out and finally stroke him, with a leap he goes a little further away.

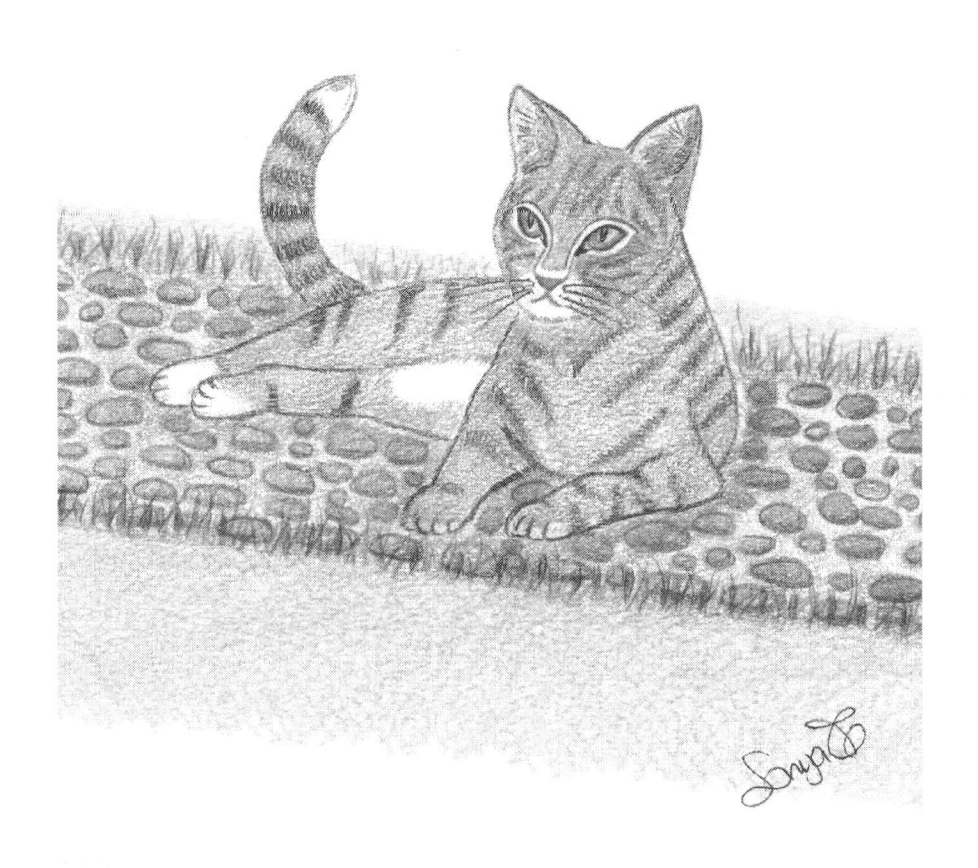

He stops, turns his back, licks himself as if I had touched him, annoyed, he looks at me, takes two or three more steps and throws himself in a strip of sun and continues to lick himself.
He's not always like this, when we are on the upstairs terrace, he is quieter and he lets me stroke him.

We are getting ready to walk home.

Great-grandmother gives my mum many pumpkin flowers, very yellow and big, so she can stuff and cook them.

I go to the basket where the flowers are, to check that we are not bringing bees home, in fact there is one inside a flower, all hairy and a little fat.

Once a bee stung me, it landed on my neck and tickled me but I didn't know it was a bee, I moved it with my hand and it stung my finger.

Now I am careful when I see them because they scare me but never as much as hornets.
Those are huge, make noise and they really hurt.

Mum has been stung once while she was picking up the laundry hanging outside the window.
Her whole arm hurt after that sting.
I jump on the way home and stop to wait for Mum because she doesn't want to jump with me.
I walk and stop, jump and stop and slowly we get home.

The children are out playing in the square so I stay with them for a long time.

They are playing "War Ball."

I wait for the game to end then the teams start it over and I join them.

We are many kids playing the game : eight on each side of the square divided by a line on the floor made with chalk.

With the ball in your hands you have to hit the opponent on the other side.

If you hit them, they become prisoners who must remain behind the game field, on the side of the square where our team is playing, we put them in the prison.

They stay there until their teammates manage to free them by making prisoners on our team.

I am on the team with Mauro, and with some of his brothers and sisters. He has many siblings, eleven or twelve.

I like playing in his team because he is the strongest and I like him too. Marcello, in the other team, is also strong and he also has many brothers and sisters.

We run a lot with this game, it's one of my favourites and when my parents call me because dinner is ready, I'm all sweaty and I would have liked to stay a little longer with the other children.

Especially now that Massimo and Lella have come out to play.

Lella is one of my favorite friends and Massimo is her brother, we always play together in the square.

I hope after dinner they are still out so I can go to play a little more until it gets dark.

When it is dark, sometimes, with Lella and Massimo we walk to the cemetery, which is behind the square, to make us shiver with fear.

It is already frightening to pass by the old Oratory.

From the keyhole you can see the dusty benches and some statues covered with white sheets.

I never went inside and I don't know why it's closed to the public.

Dad says that it could be because the structure is no longer safe but from the outside you don't see anything broken and when I play near the building I always hope that it won't collapse.

SHOES WITH HEELS AND IRON SHAVINGS

I am in grandma Peppina's basement trying on, again, the white shoes with the heels that my mum wore at her wedding.

If I found the dress, I'd wear that too, but I've never seen it.

The shoes are huge, my foot slips into the toe space and when I try to walk the shoes fall off.

But I walk there for a while, back and forth in front of the garden.

I try to run but I can't, they are just too big.

I show them to Dad who is in the workshop turning pieces of iron.

I have to be careful not to get them dirty when I go inside the garage because today the metal shavings are everywhere, but to tell the truth I have already dirtied them the previous times and since they are made of white satin I can't clean them anymore.

The shavings today are almost blue, I bend over to pick up some of them and Daddy tells me that they are made of aluminum that's why they are blue and he also says that they are sharp, to be careful not to cut my fingers.

I stay in the workshop, the smell of turned iron, machine oil, and other liquids that dad uses when he works, is strong.

I don't like that smell but now I'm used to it, it's the smell that Dad brings home in the evening before taking off the blue suit he always wears in the workshop.

He seems a little funny to me with that suit, because it's all one piece where he slips inside and then it has the buttons in front, like a baby's suit.

I'm going to take off my heeled shoes and go back to the workshop to watch Dad work and after a while I get bored and ask my grandmother if I can use her bicycle to ride to the square.

She tells me that I can, so I leave with that green bicycle which is huge for me, my feet don't even touch the ground, they barely reach the pedals.

I go fast with those big wheels, I reach the end of the square where there is the tavern and I go back and forth so many times that eventually I am tired and I go back to grandma's.

I go upstairs to drink and eat a sandwich with oil and vinegar while Dad finishes a piece of metal and then we go to our house together to wait for Mum to arrive from work.

Before leaving my grandmother's house, I open the lid of the porcelain piglet, take a handful of candies and put it in my pocket.

These are my favorites, toffee, which stick to all my teeth and palate when I eat them.

35

36

Grandma works at Fassi, which is a candies factory and she always smells like candy.

When she works she is dressed in white, like a nurse, she also has a white headset on her head and she goes to work in a white car, a Fiat 500.

I go home with dad, today the children are no longer playing, I see someone on the other side of the square walking away - Too late!

While we eat, the lady on television says they are about to start a film of cowboys and American Indians.

I ask dad if I can stay to watch the movie with him and stay up longer tonight as I don't have school tomorrow.

"Okay," says dad.

So I finish eating and I go to take the pillow from my bed. I use it to cover my face when there is a scene that I don't want to see.

I stay with dad in the kitchen and we watch the movie.

Mum doesn't like these films, she goes to the bedroom to read a Giallo Mondadori.

I always care for the Indians and I'm happy when they win.

After the film I go to bed but I stay with my eyes open for a while and the darkness starts to move, it always does that after I've been watching for a while.

Then I realise that the closet door is open and I cannot fall asleep if it is open so I call Dad who comes to close it and I also ask him to tuck the covers in.

Now that I feel safe, even though the darkness is still moving, I can fall asleep.

MY BEST FRIEND

Today I play with Betti, my best friend.

In winter I play with her almost every day because we go to school together but in summer I also do other things without her and maybe she does things with her cousins from Milan who come to visit her.

We stick green leaves to our clothes, the one that remain attached to the fabric by themselves, we do it to decorate our clothes.
I have designed a big flower with all the leaves, she has designed Betti's B all wrong and bent, so I laugh and attach her leaves a little better and so she too has to change the leaves of my design and do it better because everything one does the other must do too.

We walk up to the house of my grandmother Adalgisa.
Just before the gate there are two bushes that make long pink and even yellow flowers sometimes.
Betti and I rip them off and suck the stem.

They are sweet, we don't suck many of them because we don't know if they are dangerous, but we always do it and for now they haven't done any harm.

We walk even further, passing my great-grandmother's house. The road runs alongside the stream and is steep.

39

We reach Alessandro's house, a boy who comes to school with us, to see if he's playing outside the house.

He is there, so I ask him if we can go around the house inside the cavity between the two walls.

It is an adventure, it is a little scary, the cavity is narrow, we can only walk through because we are still small.

So we get in line, he is ahead, myself in the middle and Betti behind us, while we enter the cavity.

It's cooler between the two walls, it's a little dark, there are also cobwebs and you don't really know where you are until you go around the whole house and you can go outside again.

It's a bit like when I go around the haunted house with dad at the Funfair but not so good.

After the tour we say goodbye to Alessandro and we go back to Betti's house.

We play with Barbies.

Betti also has a Ken and a Big Jim so we can invent more stories.

But we fight sometimes because I would like Ken to be my Barbie's husband from time to time but most of the time I have Big Jim who is much shorter than Barbie.

So to make him look taller, I put Ken's trousers on him and let them dangle over his feet.

We spend almost an hour changing Barbie clothes and combing their hair.

Betti also has Barbie's yacht.

I have Barbie's bathroom and the tub makes real soap bubbles.

We make up stories by making the Barbies speak with our thin voice and Ken and Big Jim making the big voice, until the game is interrupted by Betti's aunt who calls her because dinner is ready.
So I say goodbye to everyone and I go back to my grandmother to wait for mum.

Outside the garage there is uncle Romano who has just arrived with his motorbike but has not yet parked it inside. He has a white and brown Kawasaki.
I run to him and ask him if we can take a ride before I go to my house.
He puts me up on the bike and we leave.

From behind him I scream "Let's go faster" so it accelerates and my feet vibrate on the pedals because we are going very fast and the air makes me blink my eyes when my hair blows in my face.
My hair is a short bob and it is brown and a little red when the sun hits it.

When we come back from our tour, Mum is there waiting for me a little worried because grandma told her that I had gone on the motorbike with my uncle.
My uncle helps me on to the ground.
I take Mum's hand and we go home on foot because the car has already been parked in the square where we live.

THE VINTAGE TURNTABLE

Today I am busy with the turntable which is actually a large radio a bit old with the lid that opens and underneath you can play small and large discs.

    Mom says that the little ones are called 45 rpm and the big ones are LPs.
    When I put them under the needle, being careful not to make it scrape them, I also have to change the turns with a knob otherwise they all sound strange or very fast or very slow.

    So I put 45 rpm or 33 rpm, I'm not sure what these rpm is.
    Dad says that they are those tiny lines on the discs but I still don't understand.
    Anyway, I like to play all these records, I have a full cardboard box and most of them are made of super fine and soft plastic, you can almost fold them and if they fall they don't even break.

    My favorites are Tony Dallara's Ghiaccio Bollente and Mina's Le Mille Blu
    I know who Mina is but I don't know who Tony Dallara is but they make me dance and sing.

I also have a big one LP with songs from the war period.

One of the song's title is Angelita di Anzio and that makes me cry a lot, especially when it talks about those little hands that hold the shells filled with sand but I sing the same.

And then there are some other Soldiers songs, I sing those too, they are all dad's super old records.

I also have new ones, I have Bob Marley, Marvin Gaye, Donna Summer.
My mum buys these modern ones but they sing in English.
I like music a lot but I don't understand what they say so I invent the words that resemble what they are saying, nobody understands them and I dance.

On the back of the radio there is a door and inside there are small bulbs but dad told me that they are valves and not bulbs and they are used to make the radio work.

Sometimes I call mum to come and dance with me.
It's funny when she dances, she says she's dancing the "shake" and shakes her head.
I have never seen people who dance like her, not even on television.

Dad instead teaches me to dance the waltz and the mazurka so when they have parties in the square I can dance with my friends.

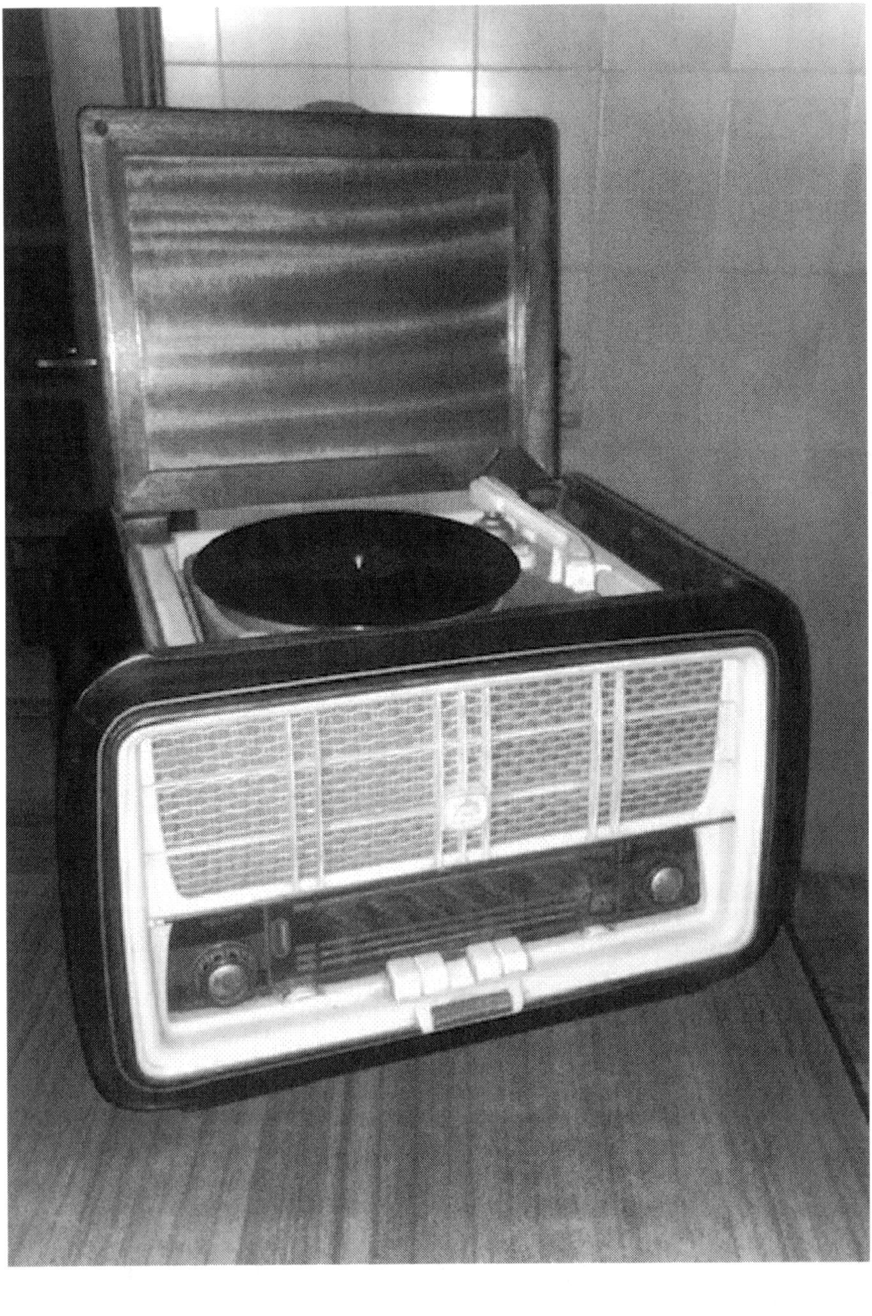

THE ROCKING HORSE AND BOXING LESSONS

Today is Sunday, I have already returned from mass, I sang at the top of my voice, I took communion, I played in the square with the children and we also had lunch.

Now I'm in my room on the rocking horse, rocking up and down.
The horse is white with an orange plush mane and tail and blue cheeks.
But I don't want the horse rocking anymore, because real horses don't rock.

I call Dad who is still in the kitchen drinking coffee and I ask him to remove the rocking frame from the horse and leave it resting on his paws.
"Then it doesn't move anymore," he says.
"It doesn't matter," I reply, "horses don't rock."

So he disassembles a few pieces and after a while the horse is resting on its hooves.
Now it seems more real even if the mane and tail are just too orange.
I climb on it and I also move it pushing it forward on the floor with the thrusts of my body.

It makes a little noise, but no one sleeps now. I am also drawing today, I draw women's faces, my mum taught me.

47

She draws these beautiful faces.

I still have to learn, mine are a bit ugly, but I fill in whole sheets until evening comes.

I go back to the kitchen, mum prepares food and dad watches television.

When Dad sees me in the corridor he says to me: "Come, I'll teach you some boxing."

I say "Okay". I always have fun with him even though many times he teaches me boy's things.

We are in the corridor and he shows me how to dodge his fists.

I lower myself, I move to the side, I step back, he always pretends with his fists, he doesn't really get close but at some point I find myself lying on the floor with my mother screaming at him "Are you stupid?".

He says "I didn't hit her hard" and helps me to get up.

It didn't hurt me, I laugh and he laughs too, but Mum got really angry so we don't play boxing anymore and we wait for the soup to be ready.

While I wait I read the new Mickey Mouse, I read first the stories of Donald Duck which I prefer.

The soup is on the table, I can see pieces floating that I don't like.

Tonight, after she got angry, Mum didn't blend the soup very well but I didn't say anything, I covered everything with grated cheese and I ate it all.

TRAVELLING BY CAR WITH THE PORTABLE RECORD PLAYER

I always get car sick when we travel so sometimes I sit in the front.

But I like sitting in the back seat with Mum because during the trip she talks with Dad a lot and I rest my head on her tummy and I can hear her voice that echoes and makes me fall asleep.

Sometimes instead, during the trip, we play games, like choosing a colour to see who counts more cars of that colour during the journey or other games where we always count things.

Or I like to sing "Fra Martino Campanaro" where first one of us starts, then the other one joins in the song and then the next person, the more you go on the more you don't understand anything anymore and everything becomes a din.

Today we are going to San Romolo for a trip to the meadows and I brought my new portable record player.
I can finally play records even when I'm away from home.

The record player is red and shiny, I'm sitting in the back seat, I brought some records and I'm playing them, happy because I couldn't wait to have a record player.

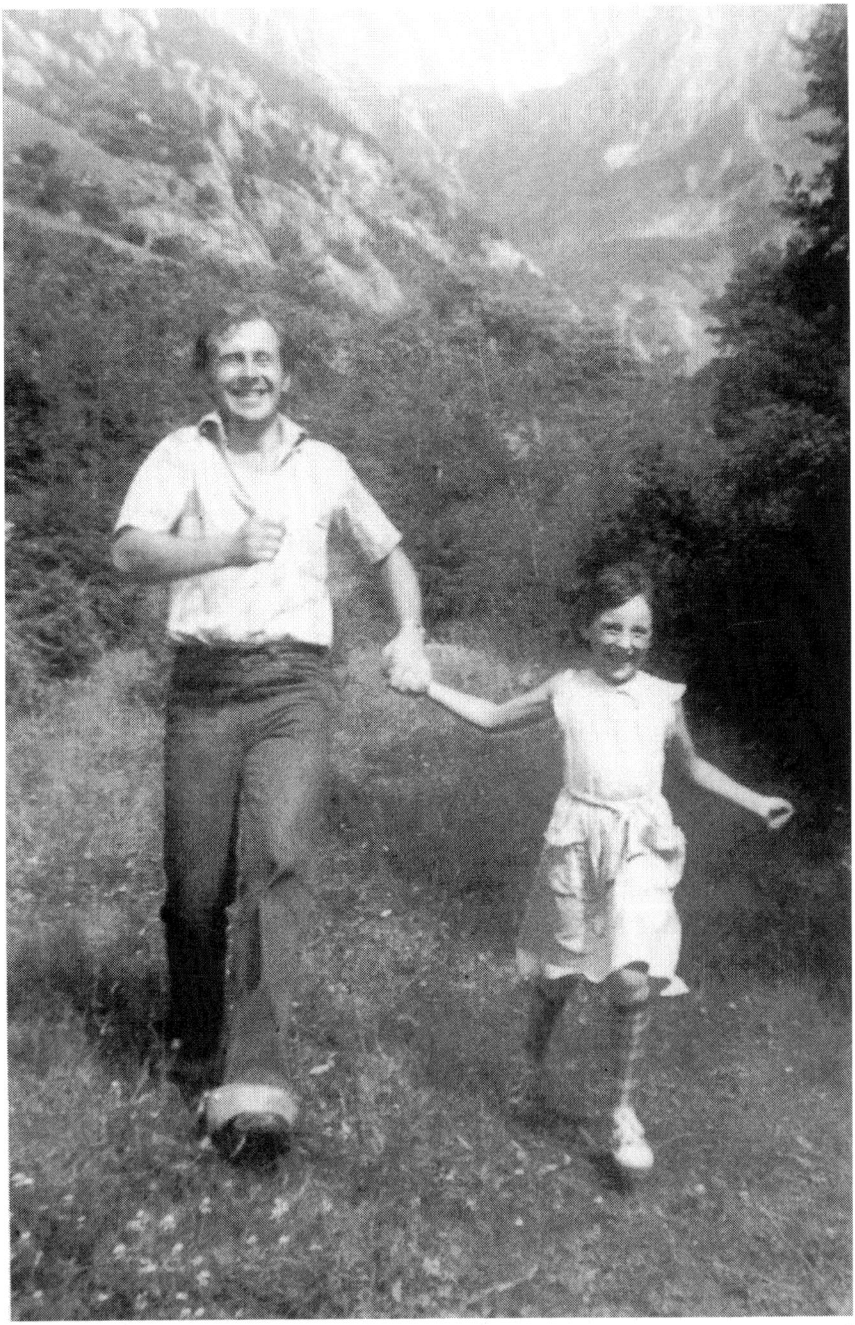

Mum is sitting in the front chatting with dad, I don't even get car sick today because I'm busy with my music.

When we go for these trips to San Romolo we always stop at the usual place to eat "Pan Bagna" which means wet bread and it is wet for real.
It is a large sandwich with tomato and basil leaves and is very good.

Then we go for a walk in these meadows, we are not far from home but we are higher and the air is fresher.
We also do downhill races with dad, hand in hand, but he runs fast with his long legs and I almost fly behind him, but he holds my hand firmly so I never fall.
While we play, Mum reads, she always reads if she doesn't work.
Dad also lets me ride him, he is on all fours, he puts a daisy on his mouth and I laugh on his back.

The afternoon passes quickly so we go back to the car and start the return journey.

I play my records again but unfortunately only for a short time because in a hairpin bend Dad has to brake suddenly and I slam the record player on the seat in front of me and the lever that spits out the records breaks.
Unfortunately there is nothing that we can do to repair the player, it no longer works.
I cry, it only lasted me one day and I can't have another.

THE SWING BETWEEN THE OLIVE TREES

Dad built a swing for me, he made it all by himself, it's iron welded together.

It does not have chains attached to the seat, but two bars that work very well.

He fixed it to a concrete base that he placed in a strip of land in the middle of the olive trees, near where our house is being built.

For now, nothing can be seen of the new house, there are excavations everywhere, concrete pillars here and there with long iron bars pointing upwards.

Today I am on my swing which brings me up, very high almost touching the leaves of the trees.//
I push myself with my legs, stretched when I go up and bent when I go down.

Dad is a little further down with other men who turn the concrete mixer, knead it and go back and forth with the wheelbarrow full of liquid concrete.

From where I am, I hardly hear the noise of the works, I hear the sound of the air in my ears as I go up and down with the swing and I also hear the birds singing when the crickets do not make too much noise.

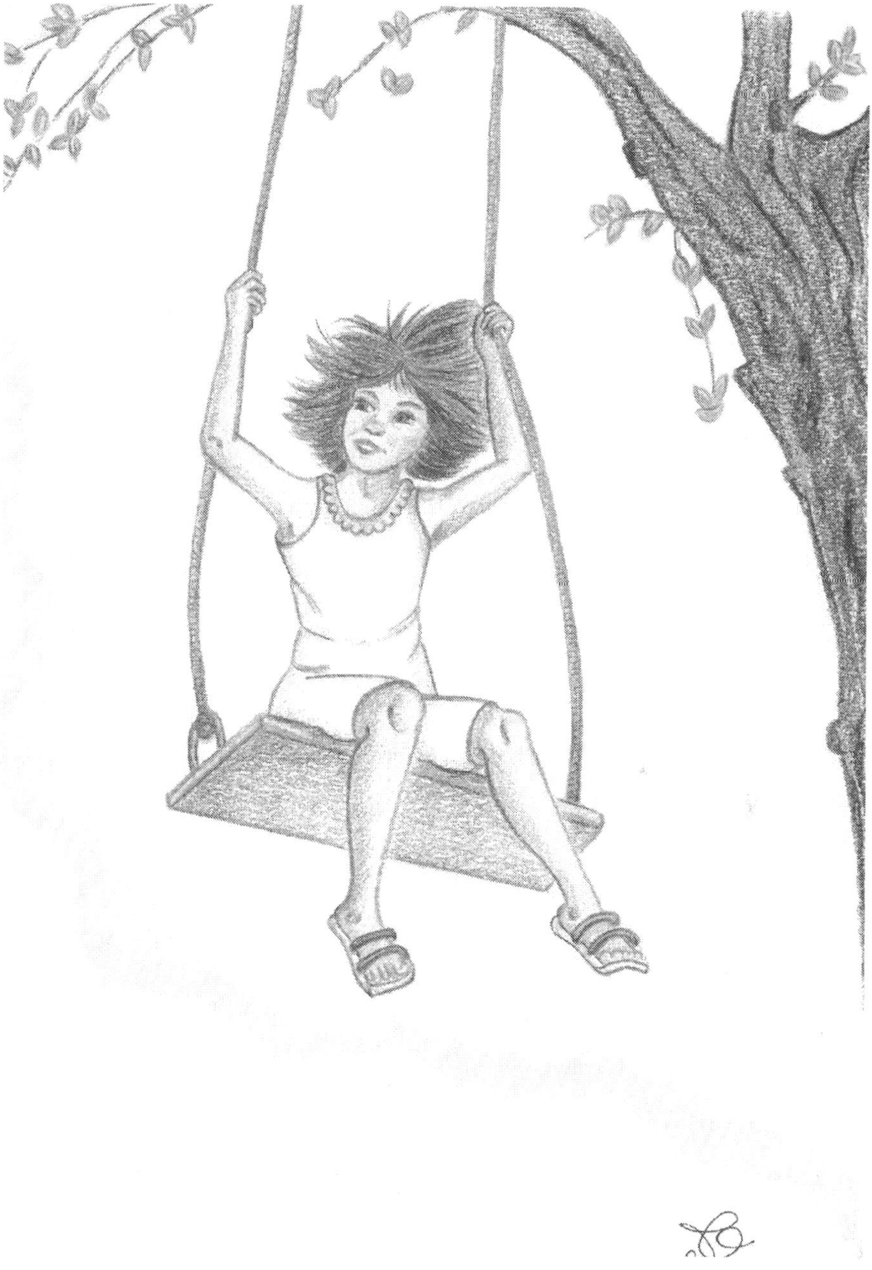

The grass is all green around me, there are country flowers scattered here and there and white butterflies flying near the swing, so we fly together.

My favourite flowers are violets, I like the perfume so much that I would eat them, but now it's too hot and there aren't any around.

I like summer, I was born in the summer, on July 3rd in a few days it will be my birthday and I can have some children come to visit to eat the cake.

A few children only, said Mum, because we live in a small house.

Dad comes to see me up here.
"Is the swing okay?" he asks me.
"It's very good! Are you pushing me up?"

And so he pushes me for a few minutes and then he goes back to work because the evening has fallen and we must soon go home.

I get off the swing and pick up some wild flowers, they don't smell, but they are colorful, Mum can put them in a vase.

I also add green leaves that don't have flowers, as they do in stores when they prepare a bouquet for you.

And then with dad we go back down the long hill that takes us to the village.

DO NOT STEAL

There are two things I do that annoy Dad.

What he can stand for a while are my fingers that with my flat hand on his arm, lift his blond hair.

He tells me to stop when he no longer wants to be treated like a cat.

The other one that drives him crazy and tells me to stop immediately is when I give him my hand and with my thumb I push his skin towards the nail of his thumb.

If I do, it leaves my hand immediately.

Now we walk hand in hand in Ventimiglia, we are going to one the Railway offices because Dad now has another job in order to earn more money to build the house.

Sometimes he still works in the garage but now he works in the electrical systems of the State Railways, a noisy place with big poles and huge cables everywhere and a room where you can control everything with many buttons and levers.

We arrive in the office and we sit on two chairs in front of this desk with a man behind it.

They talk about work and I sit for a while and then I slide down from the chair and stay there near the desk looking around me.

I find, inside an empty ashtray, many clips to hold the pages together.

I take four or five and start threading one into the other creating a small chain.

Later on the man gets up, takes us to the door and says goodbye, so we go down the stairs that lead us to the road and we start walking to the car.

After a good few metres, while we wait to cross the road, we stop at the traffic lights.

Dad moves me to the other side to make room for a man on a bicycle who leans on the pole without putting his feet on the ground.

Dad takes my other hand , the one where I still keep the paper clips, so while I move them to the other hand, he sees them and asks me: "And where did you get them from?"

"In that office in an ashtray, there were many," I answer.

"Did you ask that man if you could have them?" says dad.

"No" I reply.

"Then they are not yours, you have to bring them back" says a serious dad "You cannot take things that are not yours without asking, because then they are stolen".

I look at him and I think that the man had so many clips and he would never have noticed that four or five were missing.

But I also see that Dad is very serious and almost a little angry.

He says "Now let's go back and give them back and apologise too, okay?"

"Okay," I say and I feel a little nervous about doing this.

So we go back all the way already travelled and we are soon in the office in front of that man with my hand open to show him the clips.

I apologize and let them fall back into the ashtray, Dad also apologizes, they talk for another 5 minutes and then we go home.

He is no longer angry but I still think I did something I shouldn't have done and I go home with this thought because even though I'm a little girl I'm already a thinker.

GRANDFATHER ARMANDO

Today my grandfather Armando came to our home because I am sick with the flu and I have to stay in bed and he has to take care of me.

He lives in Sanremo alone, because my grandmother Luisa died years ago, so when my mum picks him up he is happy to spend some time with us.

He is Mum's dad, he is bald and not too tall and when he is outdoors he always wears a hat, a beret and if it is winter he also has a scarf and always wears turtleneck sweaters.

Grandad is from Tuscany, from Porto Santo Stefano and speaks with the accent of those places.

When he was young he was a sailor on the merchant ships and during those sea trips, while there was a storm, he lost part of two fingers that had remained trapped inside the hatch of the hold when the strong wind had suddenly closed it with tremendous force.

But even without part of those two fingers he can do anything including smoking so many cigarettes, that his fingers are yellowed with nicotine.

When he returns to the room, after going out to smoke again, we resume the card game.

We play different card games.

Every now and then he sings and dances because he gets tired of playing cards and the day spent in a room is really long and a bit boring.

Mum said that when he was young he was a dancer and with my grandma they would dance when he was back from his long journeys on the boat, he could stay away for months.

He also likes to go fishing and one day we went together on Uncle Romano's small boat to try to catch some fish but I remember that we didn't catch many and I had also suffered from seasickness.

Mum has arrived and prepares dinner so Grandad goes to the kitchen with her to have a glass of Rossese wine, which he likes so much. Dad makes it.

I stay in bed.

When dinner is ready Mum will bring it to me and I already imagine a plate of minced horse meat, Parmigiano Reggiano and a glass of orange juice.

All things that I need to heal quickly, according to Mum.

THE WOODEN CLOGS

Today mum works only half day because it is Wednesday so when she's back from work she comes to pick me up from grandma's and we go home together.

She goes to change her dress to start preparing food and I see that next to her bag that she left on the bench in the corridor, there is a coloured paper bag but it is closed with a stapler and I cannot see what's inside.

I go to the kitchen, turn on the TV and sit down to watch Superclassifica Show.

Mum comes into the kitchen and says "I brought you something, it's in a bag in the corridor."
" What is that?" I ask happily and run to get the bag.

I put it on a chair and start to open it, I still don't see anything because what is inside the bag is wrapped.

Then I break the paper and pull out a pair of fuchsia pink wooden clogs with high heels of my size.
I can't believe it, I put them on my feet and they fit me perfectly.

"Now be careful not to break an ankle in those heels," says mum.

I jump up and down inside the clogs, I go to my parents' bedroom to look at myself in the long mirror that is inside the door of the clothes closet.

The clogs are beautiful, I can't wait to go out and wear them.

I return to the kitchen.

Mum says, "You use the clogs at home and outside in the square, but not when we go on errands or go shopping, because you're a little girl and it would seem strange to people to see you in heels".

"Okay" I answer.

After eating I go to the square wearing my new clogs, the other girls want to try them on and I let them do it.

Then we start playing and I feel very tall and after half an hour I can also run in my heels.

When I come home after a few hours I take off my clogs and put them under the bench in the corridor and I realize that the rubber under the heels has already worn out by running back and forth.

THE SEA IN SEPTEMBER

Mum is in the bathroom washing a pile of clothes, panties and socks.

Most of the time she washes everything by hand but we have a washing machine.

While washing she always sings, even when she does other housework.

She has a repertoire of songs that I now know almost by heart but every now and then she changes the words, inventing them and I laugh.

While she is singing and washing I am getting ready because we are going to the beach.

We have to wait until at least 3 in the afternoon otherwise it is too hot and the sun burns the skin.

The beach is 20 minutes away by car and we go to Bordighera at Pippo's.

We lay down on the towels which we have put not too far from the shore.

I undress quickly and go to check the water temperature.

The pebbles are very hot, I have to run until I reach the shore and I finally have my feet in the water.

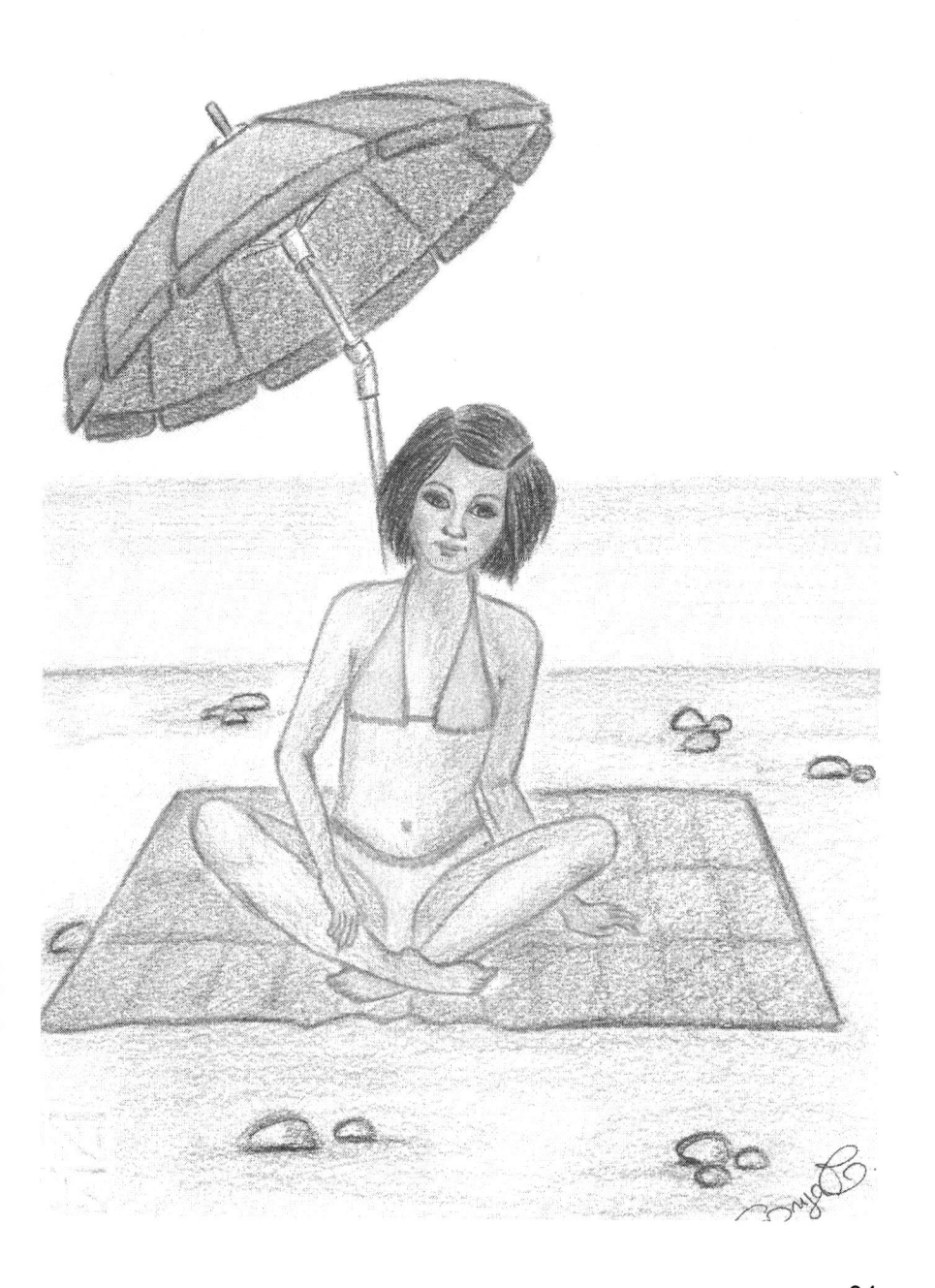

The water today is clean and clear and there are no longer many people on the beach because we are now getting towards the end of the summer.

Mum immediately starts to read her novel Giallo Mondadori and I brought myself Donald Duck's Super Almanac.

I have to wait a little longer before going to swim because I finished eating less than 2 hours ago, but with the reading the time passes quickly so I'm soon in the water.

To get myself in the water takes time because it's cool but when I am in I feel good.

I swim back and forth where I can touch the bottom with my feet because I am not very good at swimming but I dive with my eyes open holding my breath and swimming underwater.

Mum only wants to be in the water up to the top of her legs because she cannot swim at all.

She gets in the shallow water several times to cool off.

Another thing she cannot do is ride a bicycle, too bad for her.

Dad is good at cycling, he also goes to races.

Sunset comes early, we get dressed and go home all salty.

THE HARVEST

Today we went to harvest.
We are all here, Mum, Dad, Uncle Romano, Grandad Armando and Grandma Peppina, the Great-grandmother has not come, she is too old.

Dad has adorned his head with bunches of grapes and now looks like Bacchus.
I taste a few berries here and there but most of the time I play and jump from one strip of land to another.

I see my Mum and my Grandma, bent in two different rows, cutting the bunches one by one and putting them in the basket, Grandad has stopped to rest and is eating a piece of pumpkin pie that Grandma made.

I go down the hill to join my Grandad because I want to eat a piece of pie too.
Pumpkin pie is one of the best things that grandma makes, but also handmade ravioli are delicious and apple pie that has super soft sponge cake.

Dad and Uncle are loading the Ape vehicle with the baskets full of grapes and they are leaving to go to unload their load in the cellar.
While we wait for them to come back, we all rest near the cottage, in the shade to eat and drink.

Dad, Grandma Peppina and Grandad Armando

They still work until late afternoon and then, all tired, they decide to go home and finish the harvest tomorrow.

The best moment comes now that we are back in the cellar with all the grapes harvested, we wash our feet to get into the barrel to crush the grapes.
It's me, Dad and Uncle, all together in the barrel.

The stalks scratch my feet and ankles because I have the skin of a child but do nothing to Dad and Uncle.

As the grapes are crushed, we begin to go down to the bottom of the barrel, so I get pulled out and wait for them to finish because I still have one of the best fun thing of the harvest to do.

When Dad and Uncle have washed their feet and put their shoes back on, we move to the press to get more juice out of the already crushed grapes.

The press has a wheel like a rudder and attached to the wheel there is a bar that protrudes out and that serves to make the wheel turn by applying more force.

I attach myself to the bar and as the wheel turns it lifts me up and I stay until my arms no longer hold my weight.

Grandma Peppina, Uncle Romano and Grandad Armando.

LONDON-MAY 2020-LOCKDOWN

I dedicate this short collection of memories to my parents who gave me a happy and carefree childhood.

That was a period in our lives where we could only communicate through telephone calls on the landline or by writing letters on paper that were sent and then we were looking forward to receiving a reply by post.

Where children did not use computers, tablets and mobile phones to entertain themselves and others but only their own fantasy, imagination, toys and other games and we used to have a lot of fun.
Where our cheeks flushed from running, pedaling, kicking the ball, or simply for being outdoors in the sun, the wind and sometimes in the rain.
Where the messages were written on bits of paper then folded and passed under the school desks.

Today I find myself thankful for the technology, because it allows me to stay in touch with my family on a daily basis through social networks and applications on computers and mobile phones.
But when I look at the children immersed in an all-technological world I hope they are not missing something important like group play, friendship, fantasy, simple fun, the competition of a race made to see who comes first and not based on Tik Tok likes.

Although technology is now extremely important in everyone's life, I realise that it has also created a daily addiction, we are not functional without a mobile phone in your hand that we hold for most of the day and in many cases we go to sleep with our phone resting alongside on the bedside cabinet.

Personally, I wanted to take advantage of this period, without work, to draw only with paper and pencils even if the temptation to have a tablet with a drawing program was strong.

For writing I used a small notebook and my mobile phone remained untouched on the table for many hours.

While nature breathed a sigh of relief, due to the forced inactivity of almost all humanity, I also relaxed, without an alarm clock that rang every morning, without timetables to respect, without driving to go to the workplace and without daily targets to reach.

I wanted to use this period to go back in time with my memories and share, with my family and those who will read this short collection, the memories of a childhood without wi-fi.

My childhood was the happiest time of my life and I am aware of being lucky because I know that not all children had a beautiful childhood.

In 1979 my brother Giovanni was born, we have a gap of 10 years but we have many memories together: he was a little baby and then a boy and myself a young girl.

I took a lot of pictures of him, I prepared him meals, I took him to school, I played with him but he had his childhood separated from mine because of the different ages.

While he, a child, played with his friends, chasing a ball or riding a bicycle, or playing with the G.I Joe, I slowly left my child shell and started to live a new phase of my life, adolescence.

Despite two different childhoods in two different periods of time, we are still children inside and we are very close.

When we spend time together we always play games and now the age difference is no longer felt because despite being childish when together, we have really grown up.

1983 Giovanni, the stray red cat and myself.
2015 Giovanni, a different stray red cat and myself.

SUMMER 1983

It's morning and Giovanni and I are awake.
Mum and Dad are at work and I'm old enough to take care of him.

We move to our parents' bed, the sun floods the room and the day starts to be hot.
Obviously Giovanni, who is 4 years old, doesn't want to lie in bed, he wants to play.

I make him jump on the bed, holding him by the hands, and he jumps up and down trying to go higher and higher.
Up and down, up and down until those little legs lose their rhythm and he ends up lying down with his head off the mattress and unfortunately he hits the edge of the bedside table, and starts to cry.

I immediately go to check his head and see that some blood is coming out.

"Don't panic," I say to myself

I inspect the blow better while he continues to cry and looks at me to see if he has to cry more or if everything is fine.
I run to get a handkerchief in the drawer, put it on his pillow and lay him down again.

He stops crying and asks me how bad is the injury on his head and why he has a handkerchief under him.

"It is all right, everything is fine, soon the pain will go, stay down for a while" I tell him.

He looks at the handkerchief under his head and doesn't seem too convinced.

I try to stay calm in front of him and say:"I'm going to get a glass of water"

Instead I am worried and I stop in the corridor to call the supermarket where Mum works, hoping that they will get her on the phone.

After a while she comes to the phone and I explain what happened.

She reassures me immediately, I go back to the room where Giovanni is still lying waiting for me.

I tell him: "Come on if it doesn't hurt anymore we get ready, have breakfast and go outside to play.

As he gets up I check his little head again and I see that it has a small wound but the blood no longer comes out.

He looks back at that white handkerchief.

Everything is alright, this time it went well.

We get ready and then we go to the square for a little so he can ride his bicycle with the other children.

Cycling along the entire square, go back to our front door and then set off for another ride.

Accident forgotten for now...

Printed in Great Britain
by Amazon